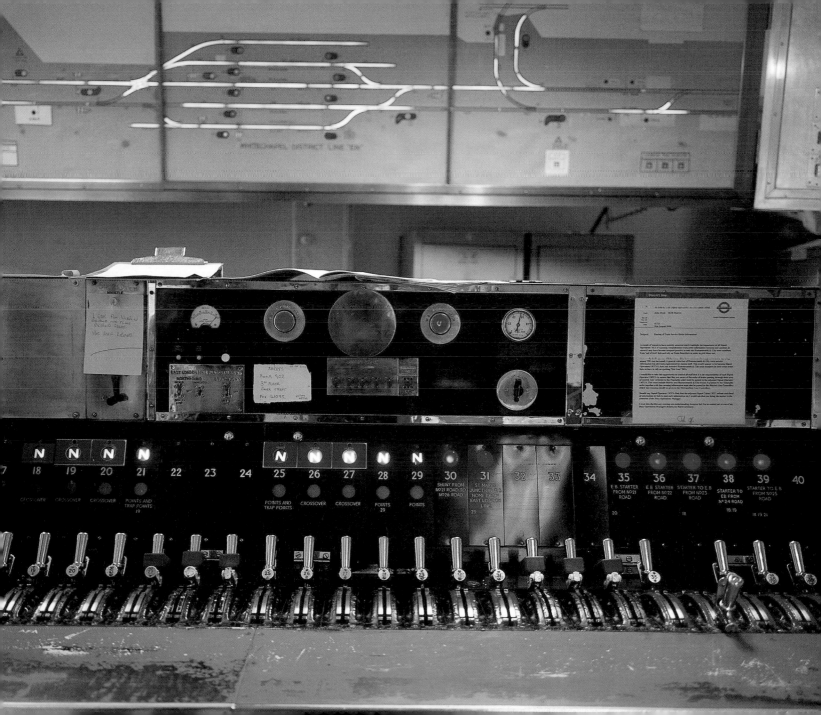

HarperCollins*Publishers*

MindtheGap

SimonJames

ForewordbyMichaelPalin

Foreword

'Mind the Gap', perhaps the most famous phrase associated with the London Underground, must surely have the creators of the system spinning in their graves. It's an acknowledgment that the thing doesn't quite work. That however fast and frequent the service, however comprehensive the network, the trains don't always fit the platforms. There's not much in it – but enough to warrant painted signs and recorded warnings.

The truth is that we English quite like it that way. We mistrust over-efficiency, and we're not prepared to put up with systems that claim to be faultless. So not only are the Underground's gaps acknowledged, they're tolerated and indeed celebrated as deficiencies that define the essentially human character of the system.

For despite the many brilliant designers, engineers and administrators who have built up London Underground over the last 140 years, the figure that matters is the three million journeys made on its network each day.

In *Mind the Gap* Simon James turns a curious and unsentimental eye on the relationship between a system and the people who use it, focusing his attention on those stations at the ends of the Underground lines, and putting faces to endearingly familiar names like Cockfosters, Upminster and Edgware.

In the spirit of gaps, and the need to mind them, James often includes evidence of damage and deficiency in his photographs. The ambitious facade of an All Day Breakfast establishment in New Cross has holes in it; a sign at Hammersmith carries an apocalyptic hand-scrawled message, 'The Last Train Has Gone'; a twisted tennis net at West Harrow suggests a degree of on-court rage that John McEnroe could only have dreamed of.

He's never predictable. He has an eye for pathos – a tube map Sellotaped to a panel at Olympia, a peeling and neglected Underground kiosk at Stanmore, a graffitied see-saw at Ruislip Gardens, the bleak and patchy Field Of Hope at Elephant & Castle. There's humour too – from now on a part of me will always associate West Ruislip with Express Denture Repairs. James shows us the mess and detritus we travellers leave behind us, alongside glimpses of the clean lines and clear design style which characterised the heyday of London Transport under Sir Frank Pick and others in the 1920s and 1930s, and which still brings a touch of glamour to the likes of Hainault and Harrow-on-the-Hill.

The Underground's admirable policy of encouraging modern architecture was continued, we see, at Newbury Park, award-winning station in the 1950s, and Stratford, one of the award-winning Jubilee line stations of the late 1990s.

Nothing in James's pictures is dressed or posed. Every subject is approached with his own oblique vision. Watford and Chesham may seduce with gabled villas and potted plants, but Kew is a canyon of graffitied concrete, Hillingdon a long, low hut that suggests it might once have been the home of some sinister wartime experiment, and the station at desirable Richmond is characterised by a cluster of signs and discarded burger-boxes.

In contrast to the depressing barrenness of the steps at Wembley Park, James creates a Hopper-like mystery at High Barnet, where the line seems sucked into dark, enclosing woodland.

There is so much to enjoy here. Simon James's vision may seem acute, odd and dispassionate, but his love for the flawed, reviled but indispensable system that ties London together underlies the whole book and gives it great character and charm.

It is very much a book about gaps, not just gaps between train and platform, but between designer and user, staff and passenger. And between dreams and reality. *Mind the Gap*, in capturing the elusive appeal of stations at the ends of the lines, gives gentle but perceptive insights into the way we live now, and particularly the elements of pride, promise, quirkiness and elegiac nostalgia that comprise the love-hate relationship we reserve only for our most important national institutions.

And the London Underground system, gaps and all, is certainly one of those.

Michael Palin
London, June 2001

Ongar The Epping–Ongar section of the Central line closed in 1994. Despite its disuse, distances across the entire system are still measured from a plate at Ongar – chosen on account of its being the furthest point on the tube from Central London, Ongar is Point Zero. I found this cleat, which would have once supported an electric rail, in the old goods yard to the south of the station. Closed 1994

Aldwych *opposite* Opened originally as 'Strand' in 1907, Aldwych station was planned as the southern terminus of the Great Northern & Strand Railway. The merger of this company with another to form the Piccadilly line put paid to this role, and the Holborn to Aldwych branch line remained underused and a historical quirk. Finally closed to passengers in 1994, Aldwych remains remarkably busy. The line is still electrified and the station is regularly used as a site for London Underground to test engineering and new signage – hence its disguise here as Mornington Crescent. Closed 1994

Ongar *left* The skeleton of a defunct roundel at Ongar. The London Underground roundel first came into existence while the various lines were separate private companies, and was developed from a similar logo used by the London General Omnibus Company. The typeface used throughout the system, Underground Sans, was commissioned by Frank Pick in 1913. At the time an absolutely cutting-edge example of a modern sans serif font, it was designed by the calligrapher Edward Johnston, who also redesigned the 'bar and disc' logo, changing it to the first version of the 'bar and circle' roundel we recognise today. The present version of the font, New Johnston, was redesigned in 1979. Both typeface and logo are the copyright of London Underground. Closed 1994

Epping *back, left* The junction of the Epping–Ongar line with the Central line. Beyond the blue plastic fence, you can just see the beginning of the Central line's electric rail. Zone 6

Wimbledon *back, right* The rolling stock on the Underground is by no means standard throughout the system. On the District line, for example, this means that it isn't possible to run direct services between Upminster and Edgware Road as the trains don't fit the lines beyond High Street Kensington. Zone 3

Richmond *left* The space beyond the buffers at the end of the District line may be littered with burger boxes and tin cans, but signs in the foreground provide a strong case for not attempting to clear the rubbish up. Zone 4

Uxbridge *right* The central bay of the three sets of tracks at Uxbridge, which are served by two island platforms. Terminus to both the Piccadilly and Metropolitan lines, the station is particularly spacious due to its need to accommodate both surface and tube rolling stock. Zone 6

North Weald The electric rail has been removed from the line between Epping and Ongar, but a stern notice beside a stile near North Weald still warns the users of a public right of way to take care crossing the line. Closed 1994

Harrow & Wealdstone *above* The northernmost point on the Bakerloo line is now the elderly mainline station at Harrow & Wealdstone. The tube stops at this platform, also a popular staging post of local pigeons, and then moves up into a siding before reversing down for the return journey. Zone 5 Kensington (Olympia) *above right* As a relative newcomer to London one of the things that fascinates me most about the city is the way its buildings come and go. These new Barratt homes are opposite the line at Kensington (Olympia). Zone 2 Richmond *opposite* A path beside the track at Richmond leads to a bridge from where it is possible to look back towards London. At the platform end of the path, almost forgotten next to a cluttered entanglement of commuters' bicycles, is the railway workers' war memorial. Zone 4

Stratford *opposite* The arrival of the new Jubilee line extension at Stratford turns the area into a major transport hub. This, along with the rejuvenation of the town centre and the arrival of 'cappuccino culture' to face down traditional East End values, is having a marked effect on house prices locally. Zone 3

Aldgate *left* This rather grand staircase leads down from the ticket hall to the concourse at Aldgate, eastern terminus of the Metropolitan line. Aldgate was one of six gates into the Roman city, originally serving the road to Colchester. The Metropolitan line, which before the advent of the East London line continued to New Cross, arrived here in 1876. Zone 1

Walthamstow Central *below left* At Walthamstow Central, by contrast, the steps up from the tube break surface next to this lonely seat on the mainline station platform. Zone 3

Ongar While looking for the old station at Chipping Ongar
I kept coming across surreal road signs to a 'secret nuclear
bunker'. This massive four-storey bunker, with three-metre
thick ferro-concrete walls, turns out to be cut into a hill
under a field at nearby Kelvedon Hatch and for the duration
of the cold war would have been the centre of government in
the event of a nuclear attack. It closed the same year as the
Epping-Ongar stretch of the Central line and is now open to
the public. Closed 1994

New Cross *left* I like the abundance of the menu at this café. You know exactly what you're going to get. Zone 2

Verney Junction *right* In 1891 the Metropolitan line arrived at Verney Junction near Buckingham, the furthest point from Central London ever reached by a London Underground line. Today you have to travel by road to get to Verney Junction. The station house is now a private residence, while another railway building across the road trades as The Verney Arms and does a very good lunch. The two platforms are overgrown with blackberry bushes, and a wicket gate leads from the track into the fields beyond. Closed 1936

Hillingdon *left* Looming large over the A40 at Hillingdon, this white metal, glass and concrete building opened in 1994 to replace the old wooden station that had been demolished for the re-routing of the trunk road. It has an integrity of design that would surely have pleased Charles Holden, had he lived to see it. In contrast, the village the station serves isn't new at all – it's mentioned in the Domesday Book. Zone 6

Whitechapel *above* The booking hall at Whitechapel has been recently refurbished; I came away convinced that the designer of the modern porch must have been a Madonna fan. Zone 2

Like most lines, the Bakerloo has evolved a lot over the years. Inaugurated in 1906 as the Baker Street & Waterloo Railway, it was soon extended to Edgware Road and Elephant & Castle, and by 1917 reached as far as Watford. Plans in the 1930s to tunnel south to Camberwell were later abandoned as too expensive. Between 1939 and 1979 the line served a second northern branch to Stanmore, now on the Jubilee line. Since 1989 the Bakerloo has served 25 stations over its 14 miles, running between Harrow & Wealdstone and Elephant & Castle.

The Central line opened in 1900 to serve London's east-west axis between Bank and Shepherd's Bush. By 1920 the line had reached Ealing Broadway. During the 1930s extensions were started to Denham (never completed due to post-war green belt laws) in the west and Ongar in the east – the tunnels of the unfinished line between Wanstead and Gants Hill were used as an aircraft components factory in the war. The line to West Ruislip opened in 1948, and reached Epping in 1949. The Central line now serves 51 stations along 52 route miles.

Epping These bungalows are at Epping, leafy eastern terminus of the Central line. The staff at Epping station are rightly proud of their garden – on the day I went to photograph there, I found a handwritten sign on the supervisor's door saying 'Welcome to Little Kew'. Outside the station, someone had planted a traffic cone into a well-tended bush. Zone 6

Wimbledon *back* Upholstered in District line livery, this seat bears the imprint of thousands of rear ends. Zone 3

Elephant & Castle *opposite* This picture taken from the traffic island opposite Elephant & Castle station illustrates the distinctive arched, ox-blood red tiled frontage that was the signature of architect Leslie Green, although this example is unusual in that the building's two terracotta facades are at an obtuse angle to each other. Green died of tuberculosis in 1908 at the age of 33 but even during his short life he made an enormous mark on the Underground. Zones 1/2

Morden *above left* One of the things that struck me when I went to photograph Morden station were these four public telephones mounted on Portland stone. Modern anti-vandal design though they are, with the continuing onslaught of the mobile they look a bit like relics for the future, waiting patiently for their museum place to be allotted. Zone 4

Richmond *left* Like the telephones at Morden, obsolescence also beckons for these mainline ticket machines at Richmond in the not-too-distant future. Touchscreen technology is already rolling out across the Underground. Zone 4

Aldwych The southbound platform at Aldwych has been shut since 1917, when Europe was a less caring, sharing community than it is today, so how this poster comes to be here is rather a mystery. A little further down the same platform is a full-size mock-up of part of the present decoration scheme for the Piccadilly line platforms at Holborn. Closed 1994

Harrow & Wealdstone *opposite* Signs warn passengers to stand well back from the edge of the mainline platforms at Harrow & Wealdstone where fast trains thunder through at high speed. A major crash occurred here in October 1952 when three trains were involved in a head-on collision. In total 112 people lost their lives, with another 150 injured. Zone 5

Hainault *left* Anyone who regularly uses the Central line will have heard the announcement 'This train is for Hainault, via Newbury Park' hundreds of times; not having been to Hainault was in fact the catalyst for my series of journeys to the ends of all the tube lines. As such it seemed that a proper respect was due to this station and I worked quite a way into the project before paying the visit. Zone 5

West Ruislip *below* Between the wars an extension to the Central line was planned to go as far west as Denham, but the Second World War put paid to this scheme, and West Ruislip remains the terminus. Zone 6

Richmond *above* Looking back to the city from the railway bridge at Richmond. Zone 4

Aldgate *above right* Aldgate station opened in 1876, and its massive roof, held up by the original iron brackets, makes it feel like a scaled-down mainline station. The inner two platforms serve the Metropolitan line, the outer two the Circle – incidentally, these are the only platforms on the network that belong exclusively to the Circle line, and they are used for regulating the timing of trains. Zone 1

Harrow-on-the-Hill *below left* This quaint curved brick waiting room at Harrow-on-the-Hill, complete with wooden benches, reminded me of films like *Brief Encounter*. Zone 5 Epping *below* I'd been hoping to find a discarded newspaper to read on the journey back from Epping but the only thing left in the carriage was this burger bag. Zone 6 Cockfosters *over* The Piccadilly line arrived out at rural Cockfosters in 1933; designed by Charles Holden, the station has remained virtually unaltered since it opened. The original shop units and signage are still intact, as well as a variety of minor details apparently left over from times past, such as wall-mounted sand buckets and an elderly intercom system, while the concrete walls have been painted in the original colour scheme. Zone 5

The first section of the District line, from South Kensington to Westminster, opened in 1868 as the Metropolitan District Railway. The line was soon extended to transport commuters from the affluent suburbs of the south-west into the centre, reaching Hammersmith in 1874, Richmond in 1877 and Ealing Broadway in 1879. From the 1890s the line started to move east, and two miles of new track from Whitechapel to Bow were opened in 1902, to give access to mainline tracks to Upminster. Today the line serves sixty stations over forty miles.

Without beginning or end, the Circle line creeps into this book by the back door. The circuit, serving 27 stations over 13 miles, first operated in 1884; almost all the service runs on other lines – only from High Street Kensington to Gloucester Road, and Aldgate to Tower Hill, are the tracks used exclusively by Circle line trains. Its tracks are known as the inner rail (anti-clockwise) and outer rail (clockwise). The line only gained its separate identity in 1949; until then the Circle was a service run by the Metropolitan and District lines.

Uxbridge *right* The tube is far from the most wheelchair-friendly public transport system in the world, although efforts have been made to make things easier in places, as is evidenced by this ramp at Uxbridge. Zone 6

Whitechapel *far right* These stairs lead to the Whitechapel staff locker room, and are made up of individual oak blocks. They don't make them like that any more. Zone 2

Wembley Park *below right* This picture of the steps up to Wembley Stadium was taken on the bleak morning after the last ever England football match under the twin towers. The wind and rain seemed to echo the result. Zone 4

Aldwych *below, far right* Since the closure of the lifts, this deep spiral staircase has been the only way down to the platforms at Aldwych. Closed 1994

Hatton Cross *right and over* Both Heathrow's stations are underground, but a good view of the runway can be found from the Hatton Cross footbridge one stop down the line. Hatton Cross station opened in 1975, while services to 'Heathrow Central', now known as Heathrow Terminals 1, 2, 3, commenced in 1977, and Heathrow Terminal 4 station opened on a single-track loop extension in 1986. Zones 5/6

West Harrow *left* Could this be the natural habitat of London's fabled White Van Man? Zone 5

Elephant & Castle *below left* Big changes are afoot at the Elephant, with major redevelopment imminent. The days of the 1960s shopping centre are numbered. Zones 1/2

Shoreditch *right* Shoreditch station is a discreet yellow-brick affair down an alleyway off Brick Lane. The single-stop, single-track branch from Whitechapel operates in peak hours only, including Sunday mornings, when the market areas of Brick Lane, Petticoat Lane and Spitalfields are at their busiest. The original entrance, designed by Charles Holden, was damaged during an air raid in 1940, although it was only finally demolished some twenty years later. Zone 2

Walthamstow Central E17 is something of an alternative destination for a big night out. The major entertainment is probably still Walthamstow dog track and the nightclub next door, but discerning diners may also like to search out L. Manze in the High Street, which serves authentic East End pie, mash and liquor in an original 1920s interior. The signage of the kiosk at the station hints at a local convergence of cultures, appearing to owe a typographical debt to Bollywood. Zone 3

Newbury Park The bus forecourt in front of the station at Newbury Park opened in 1949; its massive concrete roof was designed by Oliver Hill. The building won a Festival of Britain Award for Architectural Merit two years later and is now listed. Zone 4

Wimbledon *left* Wimbledon is one of those stations where you metaphorically seem to step over a border into London when you walk onto the platform. I like the way that the figure in the centre seems to be dissolving into the metropolis. Zone 3 High Barnet *right* This picture, by contrast, was taken looking north from the footbridge at High Barnet, and the tube lines seem to stop just short of the countryside. In actuality, the station is sited in a dip at the bottom of Barnet Hill and the countryside doesn't start until about a mile further on. Zone 5 Richmond *below right* The canopies only stretch halfway down the long platforms at Richmond. Zone 4

The Piccadilly line opened between Hammersmith and Finsbury Park in 1906, with a single-stop branch from Holborn to Aldwych added in 1907. The extensions to Uxbridge and Cockfosters both opened in 1933. The line has connected London with Heathrow Airport since 1977; a new station is planned for Terminal 5, due to open in 2007. The Piccadilly currently serves 52 stations over 44 miles, with the distinction of covering the shortest distance between any two stations on any line, the 0.16 miles from Leicester Square to Covent Garden.

The Metropolitan Railway, the world's first underground railway, opened between Farringdon and Paddington in 1863. Soon the Metropolitan extended into the untapped commuter belt to London's north-west; the line reached Aylesbury by 1892, Verney Junction by 1894 and Brill by 1899, but services beyond Aylesbury ended in 1936, and those beyond Amersham in 1961. Until electrification in 1962, the Chesham and Amersham branches were powered by steam. The Metropolitan line is actually underground for only six of its 41 miles.

Barking *right* Barking is a major interchange between the Hammersmith & City and District lines and various national rail routes. Zone 4

Upminster *far right* Life is what passes people by as they wait for their train on the platform at Upminster. Theoretically they shouldn't have to wait more than ten minutes. Zone 6

Morden This station opened in 1926 as the terminus of the
Northern Line's southwards extension from Clapham Common.
The original modernist frontage was part of a flexible Portland
stone corporate style designed for the extension stations
by Charles Holden. Originally a single storey either side of
the octagonal ticket hall, the ugly offices above the station
building were added in the 1960s. A system of overbridges
and stairs provide access to the platforms. Zone 4

Wimbledon *above* Away from the concourse Wimbledon station has a very open feel to it. Suburban Underground stations are often generous in scale, in marked contrast to those in Central London, where tube platforms connected by claustrophobic tunnels are piled on top of each other. Incidentally, the tennis happens two stops up the line at Southfields. Zone 3

Whitechapel *above right* At Whitechapel the District line, running at surface level, crosses the East London line, seen here, which runs sub-surface. While the two lines run in different directions, there's a loop at Whitechapel that means that if need be, rolling stock can be transferred from the District line to the East London line, and vice-versa. Zone 2

Chesham *left* Chesham is reached down a short branch of the Metropolitan line from Chalfont & Latimer. The Metropolitan Railway arrived here in 1889 as part of an intended route to Tring that was never completed. A steam service operated until 1962, when the branch line was finally electrified. The water tower for the steam engines still remains, along with a wooden signal box and religiously maintained garden. Band D

New Cross *below left* London Underground spend a lot of time removing graffiti, which is almost as prolific as the buddleias on the surface parts of the system. Zone 2

High Barnet *over* This instruction on the window of an empty government building in High Barnet appears to have been asking for trouble. Zone 5

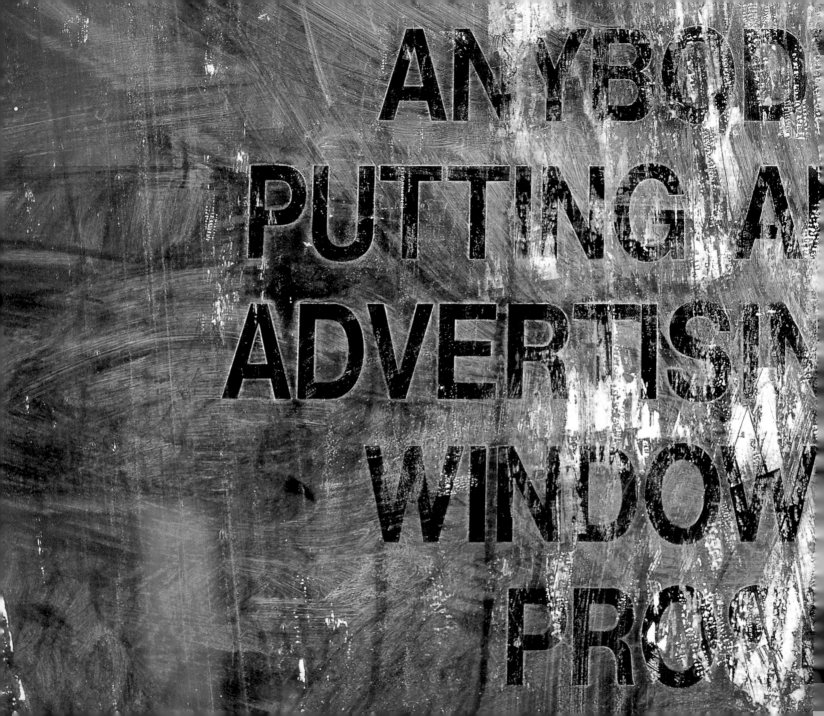

Edgware Road *above, far left* Zone 1
Whitechapel *above, centre left* Zone 2
Aldgate *above left* Zone 1
Edgware Road *below, far left* Zone 1
Aldgate *below, centre left* Zone 1
Aldgate *below left* Zone 1

The Underground is steeped in history. The earliest lines – the Metropolitan and the District – were built to mainline specifications, and ran trains that were at first pulled by steam locomotives; sub-surface lines were built by digging a deep trench along a road and then roofing it over – this is known as the 'cut and cover' method. These lines travel through clay levels that were once the surface of the city – in the central area, about three metres down, is a layer of charcoal thought to be evidence of Queen Boadicea's destruction of London in its first great fire, around 60 AD. The cut-and-cover lines are accessed by footbridges and short stairways, in contrast to the escalators and lifts that shuttle passengers to the platforms of deep tube lines.

Cockfosters Even without the trained eye of an architect, it's easy to appreciate Charles Holden's design at Cockfosters station. Now a listed building, alterations are not permitted to its structure, which is probably why the empty passimeter ticket booth sits alone amid a sea of tiles, seeming only to attract the occasional cigarette stub and used Travelcard. Passimeters were an innovation from the United States that were introduced in the late 1920s to speed passenger flow and only phased out in the 1980s with the introduction of a new ticketing system. Zone 5

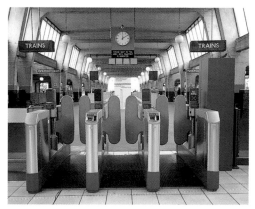

Opened in 1869 as the East London Railway between Wapping and New Cross Gate, the East London line runs through Sir Marc Brunel's twin tunnels under the Thames. Construction of these road tunnels had started in 1825, but funds to build access ramps down to them never materialised, and in 1843 they opened to pedestrians only, surviving as a curiosity until bought by the railway in 1865. The line nowadays serves nine stations over five miles, from Whitechapel to New Cross and New Cross Gate, with a limited service to Shoreditch.

The Hammersmith & City line only gained its own identity in 1990, having until then been part of the Metropolitan line, and grew out of the 1863 cut-and-cover railway between Farringdon and Paddington. The western section to Hammersmith opened in 1864, while the line reached its current eastern terminus at Barking in 1936. The line shares rolling stock with the Circle line, housed in a depot at Hammersmith that was built in 1906, when the line was electrified. Today the Hammersmith & City line serves 28 stations over 16 miles.

Whitechapel I went to Whitechapel on a Sunday morning and was shown round by the friendly supervisor. It was obvious he took a huge pride in the Underground and its heritage. Before being taken off to see the oak-block staircase and the signal box, one of the last manually-operated ones on the system, I noticed this old map pinned up in his office. Zone 2

The East London line 1998

HISTORICAL MAP OF THE UNDERGROUND RAILWAYS

DESPATCH
PLEASE TAKE
LETTERS OUT OF
BAG ON ARRIVAL

Aldwych *back and left* The picture here and the two on the previous pages were taken in the tunnel that runs underneath Kingsway between Aldwych and Holborn on this disused dogleg of the Piccadilly line. The temperature is pretty constant this far below ground, the darkness absolute and there's no sound apart from your shoes on the gravel between the sleepers. From Aldwych it takes about ten minutes to walk up the line to where a train now used for engineering tests and the occasional film part is stored. Closed 1994

Barking Historically Barking was a fishing port, with the industry in the nineteenth century employing over a thousand people in boats known as 'Barking smacks'. The writer Daniel Defoe remarked on the durability of these vessels and their darker use as 'press smacks', sent up the coast to press sailors into the navy in time of war. The railway arrived in Barking in 1854; today the Hammersmith & City line ends here, the District line passes through on its way to Upminster, and there are connections with mainline routes. Zone 4

New Cross *far left* New Cross today houses a mixed community, including the famous Goldsmiths' College, which until 1889 was the Royal Naval School. Zone 2

Barking *left* Graffiti is a real problem throughout the tube. Occasionally you see an impressive example of the art. This old carriage is not one of those. Zone 4

Mill Hill East *below, far left* Here I found myself wondering if lost dog and cat notices pinned to telegraph poles ever actually result in the return of peripatetic pets. Zone 4

Hammersmith *below left* The nightly announcement to late revellers that the last train has gone must have been cause for much grief over the years. Zone 2

Hainault *above left* Sometimes photography enriches even the most banal of subjects. In this case the film has brought something special out of the subdued colours of the bricks and the first aid cupboard. I'd like to know when the stretcher was last used. Zone 5

Cockfosters *above* Charles Holden's sub-surface booking hall at Cockfosters, with its vaulted ceiling, concrete buttresses, original globe light fittings and generous expanse of tiles on the floor, looks to all intents and purposes the same as it did on the day it opened. Zone 5

Walthamstow Central *right* It's interesting to note that religion is considered something worth proclaiming from the walls in Walthamstow – the area is thought to have once been a safe haven, or 'stow', for pilgrims on the ancient road to Waltham Abbey. Zone 3

Edgware Not to be confused with Edgware Road, Edgware is one of three northern termini of the Northern line, the Underground having arrived here in 1924. Edgware station isn't the most attractive of places to photograph, but even here the fabric of the building alludes to its past. Zone 5

Until the 1960s, no brand new tube line had been started for more than fifty years; plans for the Victoria line dated back to 1937, but work didn't start until 1962. The first stretch, from Walthamstow Central to Highbury & Islington, opened in 1968, and the line reached Brixton in 1971. From the start, the line has used the Automatic Train Operation system, with signal checks, acceleration and braking all controlled by a central computer. Serving 16 stations, the Victoria is the only true 'tube' line, submerged for the whole of its 14 miles.

The Fleet line, as the Jubilee was originally to be called, was planned to run between Stanmore and Lewisham. Tunnelling started in 1971, and the line opened between Stanmore and Charing Cross in 1979. The green light to extend southwards was not given until 1993, by when an extension to Docklands had become more economically viable, and the Green Park to Stratford stretch opened in 1999. Between Canada Water and Canning Town, trains cross the river three times in three stops. The line now serves 27 stations over 24 miles.

Ruislip Gardens *left* This see-saw is in the park next to Ruislip Gardens, near the western end of the Central line. Fifty yards further on I found the burnt-out skeleton of a stolen motor scooter lying amid discarded sweet wrappers that suggested the age of those responsible. Zone 5

West Harrow *right* This picture and the one on the first page of the book were taken on the same bright spring morning at West Harrow. In spite of the traffic cones in the boating pond, the area around the station still sits well within the myth created by John Betjeman's Metroland. The Metropolitan line divides the park and tennis courts from well-tended allotments where vegetables were growing in neat rows. Zone 5

Hillingdon *left* The view from the eastbound platform. I like the effect of the silver birches against the blue paint. Zone 6
Kew Gardens *below* A bridge over the Richmond branch of the District line – not a view you'd somehow expect at Kew Gardens. Zones 3/4
Amersham *over, left and* High Barnet *over, right* Across the outer limits of the network an indicator as to the line on which you're travelling can often be found in the style of the footbridges. Band D *and* Zone 5

West Ruislip *left* Tourist information at West Ruislip – a poster reveals details of local attractions. Zone 6

Ongar *below left* The Ongar section of the Central line closed in 1994 but was recently purchased by the Epping–Ongar Railway with the intention of re-opening the line as a single-track shuttle. I was given a ride in their diesel engine as far as Epping, and on the way back took this picture of Ongar station from a low loader wagon on the front of the train. Jim the driver kindly 'zoomed' me backwards and forwards until the framing of the shot seemed right. Closed 1994

Mill Hill East *below right* Mill Hill East is one of the few stations where you have to go upstairs to catch the tube. Incidentally, Greenford, on the western stretch of the Central line, is the only place on the network where you need to take an escalator up to the Underground. Zone 4

Edgware Road The track here runs along an original stretch of the Metropolitan Railway. Edgware Road station is at the junction of the busy Edgware and Marylebone Roads; it's not much to look at from the outside, but hides some interesting details behind the dull facade. The workings of the tube, including the plentiful electrical wires, are particularly exposed in this picture. Zone 1

Edgware Road *far left* The entrance of the Hammersmith & City line station building, designed by Charles Clark and opened in 1928. Zone 1

Edgware Road *left* A subway leads down to the Bakerloo line, again at Edgware Road. Unusually, the Bakerloo and the sub-surface lines are served by completely separate buildings here; the Bakerloo's dates from 1907 and has a facade by Leslie Green. Zone 1

Watford *below, far left* Designed in Arts and Crafts style by Charles Clark, Watford station opened in 1925 and to some extent realises the ambitions of the tube's late Victorian entrepreneurs. Here the Metropolitan line fetches up in the middle of a neatly maintained suburban housing estate known as Cassiobury Park, about a mile from the town centre. The Metropolitan line was well known for encouraging building on green field sites – uniquely, the company was permitted to hold on to property for its own developments, rather than being obliged to sell off any surplus land not needed for the railway. Perhaps the greatest property speculator in the Underground's history was Charles Tyson Yerkes, who had amassed phenomenal wealth from streetcar operations in his native Chicago. He arrived in London in 1900 and by the time of his death five years later controlled the entire system, with the sole exception of the Metropolitan line. Band B

Stanmore *below left* The tube system is in a state of constant evolution, with routes chopping and changing over the decades. Stanmore, for example, started out as the end of the Metropolitan branch line from Wembley Park. In 1939 the branch was transferred to the Bakerloo and since 1979 it has been part of the Jubilee line. Zone 5

Ongar *above* At Ongar a diesel-powered train complete with guard's van awaits permission to restart the shuttle service connecting with the Central line, although a requirement to build a new platform at Epping currently prohibits this from happening. Closed 1994

West Ruislip *right* West Ruislip is the terminus of the longest possible continuous journey on the Underground, the 34 miles from Epping, which will take you an hour and a half. Zone 6

Edgware *opposite* Edgware station has a rather charmless shed-style corrugated roof, underneath which details such as these precisely-built wooden benches in their panelled alcove hint at its past. Zone 5

Wembley Park Closest station to the twin-towered stadium, Wembley Park is well known to anyone who follows football. At the turn of the twentieth century, however, the area was the site of a tower that became known as Watkin's Folly. In 1889 Sir Edward Watkin, one-time Chairman of the Metropolitan Railway, chose Wembley Park as the site for an iron, eight-legged tower intended to reach the height of 350 metres and dwarf the one in Paris. Gustave Eiffel himself turned down an offer to build this proposed addition to the London skyline, and Sir Benjamin Baker, engineer of Scotland's Forth Bridge, was taken on instead. The project ran out of money when the tower was only sixty or so metres from the ground, and construction was abandoned; in 1907 the foundations were cleared using dynamite. Here we're looking back towards Wembley Park station, from the balcony above the stadium steps. Zone 4

Stanmore *below left* Zone 5
Epping *above left* Zone 6
Ruislip Gardens *above* Zone 5
West Ruislip *right* Zone 6
Green meets grey at the ends of the lines. I've always been interested in borders. The arbitrary places which define the end of one thing and the beginning of something else often seem to harbour a visible tension.

Aldwych *back* It was the lifts that finally put paid to Aldwych station – it would have cost £3 million to refurbish them, so instead the single-stop branch from Holborn was closed. Seeing the hand-operated doors on these old Otis lifts, which date from 1906 and are now permanently moored at the tops of their shafts, rekindled vivid memories of my first trips to London as a five-year-old, when a ride on a lift was almost as exciting as a ride on a train. Closed 1994

Elephant & Castle *left* One of the Elephant's greatest claims to tube fame dates from 1924. Although there were numerous births later among those sheltering on station platforms from wartime bombs, there is only one recorded instance of a birth actually occurring in the carriage of a tube train. Thelma Ursula Beatrice Eleanor (note her initials) was born prematurely on a Bakerloo line train at Elephant & Castle, her mother assisted by station staff. Zones 1/2

Verney Junction *right* After lunch in The Verney Arms, supervised by a ginger cat that could have escaped from *Alice in Wonderland*, I went looking for the old station. Through a gate that was once a level crossing are the remnants of two platforms, a turnstile and a set of rails vanishing off into the undergrowth. This is the view towards London. Closed 1936

Stratford *back, left* At the other end of a short subway from the elderly Central line platform at Stratford is the elegant terminus for the new Jubilee line extension, which connects the East End to Docklands and the South Bank and opened in 1999. The Anglo-Italian architect Roland Paoletti supervised the design of all the extension stations; not since the work of Charles Holden in the 1930s has new architecture on the tube received such widespread critical acclaim. Zone 3

Hatton Cross *back, right* Heathrow has a heritage of its own. This building is at the eastern end of the runway near to Hatton Cross station. Zones 5/6

Theydon Bois *above left* I made several trips out to the eastern end of the Central line. The tube here is just leaving the village of Theydon Bois on its brief journey across the M25 to Epping. I'm told quite a few London taxi drivers choose to live in Theydon Bois. Zone 6

Cockfosters *below left* The Piccadilly line reached Cockfosters in 1933, inspiring a building boom in this relatively rural area, and new housing estates were laid out on what had up till then been open fields. However, any expansion further north was prevented by the green belt legislation of the 1950s. London ends abruptly by the junction of Cockfosters Road and Chalk Lane, giving way to farmland. Zone 5

Newbury Park *right* Oliver Hill's early commissions were country houses and gardens designed in the Arts and Crafts style – he was a friend of Edwin Lutyens. But in the 1930s Hill turned towards modernism, favouring curved lines, as shown here in his bus forecourt at Newbury Park, built in 1949. Zone 4

New Cross Gate The southbound East London line service alternates between its termini at New Cross and New Cross Gate stations, a few minutes' walk away from each other. Leaving these stations for central London, it's usually quicker to jump on a mainline train heading for Charing Cross. Zone 2

Mill Hill East *left* The Northern line was only extended to Mill Hill East, at the end of a single-stop, single-track branch from Finchley Central, to serve nearby Inglis Barracks during the Second World War. The platform is high up and gives a good view of the suburbs it connects with the centre. The viaduct that carries the line over Dollis Brook marks the Underground's highest point above street level, at twenty metres. In the quest for ends of the lines it's one of those satisfying termini that ends properly, with a set of buffers. Zone 4

Hainault *below left* Platform I at Hainault is virtually unchanged since the station originally opened in 1903 as a branch line of the Great Eastern Railway; Platform 2, however, was rebuilt in the late 1940s in a more modernist style for the new Central line service. This is Platform 2, enhanced just a smidge with the wide-angle lens. Zone 5

Edgware Road *above* Four lines intersect at Edgware Road, making it possible to go direct to any number of destinations; although ironically Edgware isn't one of them. Zone 1

Edgware *above right* The end of the Northern line at Edgware. The black tunnel beyond the platform doesn't lead anywhere, and is a relic of plans in the 1930s to extend the line as far as Bushey Heath, a project that was scrapped with the green belt legislation following the war. The trains stop immediately in front of it before reversing back towards Morden. Zone 5

Ealing Broadway *left* The end of the Central and District lines. For a short while, from 1883 to 1885, the District line ran all the way to Windsor, via Ealing Broadway. Zone 3

High Barnet *right* Sidings at High Barnet bring Northern line trains to a satisfying full stop. Zone 5

Aldwych Strand station became Aldwych in May 1915 to avoid confusion with the Northern line station at Charing Cross, which was renamed 'Strand' the same day. Aldwych station has two platforms, although the one in this picture has not been used for nearly a century; you can just make out the old name on the wall. The station was closed for almost the entire duration of the Second World War, when it operated as a public air raid shelter. There are around forty of these so-called 'ghost stations' on the network. Closed 1994

Ongar *above* Discarded bolts in the goods yard at Ongar. The
station's approaches may have been downgraded to a taxi rank
but reminders of its former glory sit quietly, ready for the
re-opening of the line one day. Closed 1994
Verney Junction *above right* Slowly but inevitably, nature
reclaims the platform at Verney Junction. Closed 1936
Wimbledon *opposite* A District line train at Wimbledon awaits
its signal to make the journey back to Earl's Court. Zone 3

Brixton Another Saturday morning and more heavy rain; this time at Brixton, one of the hipper places on the planet, where the weekend was in full swing. Immaculately dressed representatives of the Nation of Islam were selling their paper on one side of the station entrance, while members of the Socialist Workers Party controlled the opposing wall. Both parties ignored with considerable dignity the manner in which they were being drowned out by the megaphone message of an evangelist group a little further down the road. None, I suspect, would have been tempted by the tiny tart's card in the phone box in front of the station, which appealed to instincts on an altogether baser level. Zone 2

Uxbridge From its style, and the elegant way in which its step
has been integrated into the station platform, this penny
weighing machine appears to be an original feature of the 1938
Uxbridge re-design; the original station had opened in 1904
and was situated where the sidings are today. The slot looks
like it has been blocked up since decimalization changed the
shape of the coinage in 1970. Zone 6

Stratford The state-of-the-art architecture of the new
Jubilee line extension has re-established the Underground's
position as a century-long pioneer of cutting-edge design; the
development at Stratford is by Chris Wilkinson Architects.
Photographing this wing-like structure, made from extruded
aluminium, I found myself wondering what Charles Holden
would have done with the materials now available. Zone 3

ACCESS
PROHIBITED

Uxbridge Opened in 1938, the new station at Uxbridge was designed by Charles Holden and Leonard Bucknell – a poured concrete cathedral complete even to the inclusion of stained glass by Ervin Bossányi (depicting the coats of arms of Uxbridge Urban District Council and the counties of Middlesex and Buckinghamshire). Clerestory windows and circular ones in the roof allow light to drop in pools into the spacious booking hall. Similarly to Cockfosters, Holden has elected to leave the board marks of the poured concrete visible, emphasising the functional nature of the structure. Zone 6

Kensington (Olympia) The single-stop branch of the District line from Earl's Court to Kensington (Olympia) serves the show halls immediately opposite, with trains running every 15 minutes. The first hall, originally called the National Agricultural Hall, was re-named Olympia when it began staging circus spectaculars in 1886. Zone 2

Upminster The day I went to Upminster it was very cold, blowing a gale and belting with rain. My golf umbrella broke in the wind and I got soaked; but the rain on the tarmac made the colours glow in the camera. Between 1910 and 1936, District line trains ran on a limited timetable beyond Upminster all the way to Southend; this day, though, would have been far from ideal for a seaside excursion. Zone 6

Whitechapel *opposite* A peculiarity of the Circle line is that due to its circular route, the wheels of its trains tend to wear unevenly. To combat this problem, one Circle line train per day travels on from Tower Hill to Whitechapel, then reversing back to Liverpool Street, a manoeuvre that turns the train round to put wear on the opposing set of wheels. Zone 2 Uxbridge *left* The platforms at Uxbridge are currently undergoing renovation. Zone 6

Amersham At the end of the Metropolitan line, Amersham is situated in Buckinghamshire's Chiltern hills. It carries the distinction of being the highest station on the Underground network, at 150 metres above sea level, as well as its most westerly point, 27 miles from Central London. Band D

Minding the Gap

From its earliest days the Underground has been viewed with a certain ambivalence by Londoners. The world's first underground railway, the 'cut and cover' Metropolitan Railway, opened in 1863. Perhaps prompted by the three-metre-deep flooding it received from the Fleet Sewer just before it opened to the public, it quickly became known as the Drain. On balance, however, the convenience of the new mode of transport outweighed passengers' misgivings and it was a huge success. The first proper 'tube' line, the City & South London Railway, opened from King William Street to Stockwell in 1890, transporting its customers in claustrophobic, windowless carriages they nicknamed padded cells. The passengers' psychological need for windows (despite there being nothing to see out of them) had not yet been recognised.

London is now a vast, sprawling metropolis. Some of its boundaries long predate the Underground system, such as the ancient ramparts still visible in a few places and the sites where grisly roadside gibbets once terrified visitors into obeying the law. Others, such as the North and South Circular roads and that car park known as the M25, are more recent, but the tube map provides one of the most relevant definitions of the city's reach. Modern London certainly makes no parochial demands that its citizens be born within earshot of Bow Bells. Today it's a truly international city drawing its population from the four corners of the globe, with hundreds of languages spoken across its pavements, parks and public spaces; yet it still feels English through and through. Londoners, to the point of cliché, often describe the capital as a city of villages where you can pop into the pub or corner shop, find a cheery welcome, and know the name of the person serving you. Road traffic in the metropolis, by contrast, is dysfunctional: gridlock threatens, and outbursts of road rage seem increasingly common. But London's many villages, divided by distance and the river, are bound firmly together by its ageing public transport system. Without the Underground, London would grind to a permanent halt in a matter of hours.

Newcomers to London first have to learn how to get about, not necessarily the simple issue of geography it sounds. Time and distance, for instance, are measured differently within the capital. In terms of mileage alone Londoners may not have that far to travel to work, but millions endure a long journey at either end of the day. The notion of a nine-to-five lifestyle doesn't really exist in the same way that it does in provincial towns.

For the majority of its passengers, the tube just *is*. It forces them into closer-than-comfortable contact with fellow humanity, breaks down increasingly frequently, is delayed increasingly regularly, is too hot in summer and too draughty the other 360 days of the year. For some it provides the portal to a family day out, a night of love or a flight to the sun. Others find in it a brief period of shelter and warmth. For a sad few, known as 'one-unders' in tube-speak, it offers an escape from this world altogether.

More than three million journeys are made on the tube every working day, but the majority of these are within the central zones. For most travellers, distant locations such as Cockfosters, Morden and Upminster are of little consequence; these places, if they exist at all, have a conceptual rather than a physical life, prompted only then by illuminated destination boards and the unremitting automated litany of train Tannoy systems. In my own journeys, I became more and more fascinated with the names of these mysterious places. Finding myself filled with a diluted version of the same spirit of adventure that moved Columbus and Cook to cross the oceans, I began making trips to the ends of the lines and photographing what I found there. Captain Cook, incidentally, turns out to have lived near Mile End tube station, but they hadn't built it at the time.

This morning's journey begins right in the middle of the system, on a crowded platform twenty-six metres below the mid-morning bustle of Oxford Circus. To the consternation of fellow travellers, I've just managed to squeeze aboard the crammed carriage. Central line trains have been described as a very effective way of fitting a quart into a pint pot – at capacity their eight cars will carry 1,652 passengers through tunnels four metres in diameter (272 seated, the other 1,380 envious). Heads bow in unison, allowing the curved doors to close fully at the third attempt. Space exists only above shoulder level, and this quickly fills with a familiar atmosphere – a simmering incongruity of perfumes, bad breath, body odour and stoic disgruntlement, seasoned with the slow-fuse fizzing of personal stereos. Londoners, adhering to tube etiquette, determinedly ignore each other, looking at anything and everything except the eyes of the passenger three inches in front of them, while tourists, who don't know any better, chatter away obliviously.

The carriage lurches forward and an automated voice dangles temptation before her captive audience: 'This train is for Epping. The next station is Tottenham Court Road.' Epping is almost twenty miles away and, barring any delay, the journey should take about fifty minutes. Eduardo Paolozzi's Modernist mosaics at Tottenham Court Road are followed (though you wouldn't know it) by British Museum station, which closed in 1933 and in the darkness offers few clues to its existence. Since surface alterations some years ago this station is now accessible only by walking the seventy or so metres back along the line from the platform at Holborn. Its original fittings are said to be intact, sealed in soot and awaiting a future generation of archaeologists.

The screeching of wheels on sharply curving tracks brings reality back into the frame at Bank, in this dress-down age still a bastion of the grey pinstripe suit. The tube is many things to many people, and different moods prevail at different times of day. Commuters dominate until about 10am, a sober group who grudgingly share the last half-hour with tourists wishing to squeeze the full value from their one-day Travelcards. A mixed crowd of daytime travellers then co-exist alongside a constant flow of transit passengers, moving between Heathrow and the mainline railway stations, until the late-afternoon rush. From 5pm till 7pm, weary commuters retrace their steps home, and then a more bohemian ambience permeates the tunnels.

At Liverpool Street, the crush eases and seats are freed up. Pastimes other than gasping for the occasional breath are now possible. Time judders by unnoticed in the darkness of the tunnel; the mind wanders. In another dimension the Underground journeys through the detritus of times much longer past. Near Liverpool Street, for example, the Central line runs roughly parallel to the city walls. This is the oldest part of London, first settled by the Romans soon after the conquest in AD 43. In those days the area just beyond the city walls was a cemetery, burials not being permitted within the city. Building projects around what is now Spitalfields still occasionally unearth the remains of residents of Londinium.

Beyond the City lies the East End, which was bombed almost flat in the Second World War and has long offered a first home to newcomers to London. Jews, expelled from the realm by Edward I in 1290, were re-admitted to England by Oliver Cromwell in the seventeenth century. The Spitalfields area soon became known for its skilled craftsmen, an association boosted by the arrival of the Huguenots, fleeing religious persecution in France; weavers and dyers intermingled with brewers and metalworkers. The Whitechapel Bell Foundry, where Big Ben was cast in 1858, is still working today and Brick Lane, renowned for its bagel bakeries, is these days at the heart of a thriving Bangladeshi community.

Daylight floods the carriage as we surface at Stratford: from now on it's overground all the way to Epping. Stratford may have been mentioned in *The Canterbury Tales*, but it's here that we bump briefly into the future. Next to the scruffy old Central line platform, an elegant aluminium and glass terminus serves the new Jubilee line extension. The architecture of this part of the Jubilee line has been much trumpeted, but an excellence of design has always been part of the tube experience. The stations at Uxbridge, Cockfosters, Southgate and Hillingdon all speak volumes for the vision of London Underground at its best. The work of Leslie Green, whose signature ox-blood red tiling still faces so many stations, and Charles Holden, who designed Southgate, Piccadilly Circus and the company headquarters at 55 Broadway, well stand the test of time. Other undersung heroes include Harry Beck, designer of the tube map and Sir Frank Pick, who began his career as a booking clerk in 1902, eventually rising to become Chief Executive of the London Passenger Transport Board. It was Pick who, in 1913, commissioned the distinctive Johnston corporate typeface and the redesign of the symbol that became the famous roundel.

The industrial revolution reached Leyton, beyond Stratford near the river Lea, at the beginning of the nineteenth century, when large tracts of local marshland were drained for commercial use. Here the landscape starts to look more suburban than urban, and the trains pick up a rattling pace between the further-spaced stations.

Beyond Leytonstone, the Hainault branch line cuts back underground for the five-mile stretch through Wanstead, Redbridge and Gants Hill before breaking the surface again near Newbury Park. During the Second World War these tunnels were transformed into an aircraft component factory; extra entrances were dug for the two thousand workers and a narrow-gauge railway installed for moving materials and completed parts.

Back on the Epping branch, Snaresbrook, South Woodford and Woodford pass quickly. At the next stop they're still trying to live down what the national press dubbed the 'Buckhurst Hill Alien', when a 'foetus' found at the station caused chaos but turned out to be no more than a child's toy that had been left on the platform. Then comes Loughton, for centuries an important stop on the old road to Cambridge. Today Loughton is perhaps best known for the high-security Bank of England Printing Works beside the railway, where all English bank notes are printed, nearly a billion of them a year, which explains the razor wire along its perimeter.

This far-eastern stretch of the Central line came into existence as a result of the nationalisation of the railways in 1948. Until then the track was part of the London & North Eastern Railway; electrification only reached Epping in late 1949. The tube makes one of its two breaks through the M25 between Theydon Bois and Epping (the other is on the Amersham branch of the Metropolitan line). Epping station itself feels like something of a throwback – an elderly footbridge connects the two platforms and a steam train puffing around the corner wouldn't appear in the least bit out of place. Until its demise in 1999 the annual station gardens competition was fiercely contended across the outer reaches of the network, and more than customary care still goes into the plantings here.

Central line trains now terminate at Epping, but it's not one of those termini that ends with a set of buffers: the rails continue under the footbridge, under the road bridge and on into the litter-strewn distance. Until 1994 Epping was three stops short of the end of the line: a single-track shuttle service continued on to Chipping Ongar, stopping off at North Weald and Blake Hall on the way. Although no longer electrified, the track still connects with Ongar and the stations and a signal box remain. The closed section was recently bought by the Epping–Ongar Railway, with the intention of reviving the service. The new company currently operates occasional trips down the line but is required to stop short of Epping station at the blue plastic fence that marks their border with London Underground territory. Safety regulations demand the building of a new platform at the Epping end of their track before the service can be resumed.

Perhaps unsurprisingly, the ends of the tube lines are just as varied as the rest of our chequered landscape. Some, like Watford, terminate in Betjemanesque leafy suburbs while others are more ambiguous borderlands, not quite city, not quite country, where tendrils of the metropolis penetrate the pastures beyond. Such places sometimes harbour mystery. Close to Chipping Ongar, for example, is the secret nuclear bunker from which the remains of the nation would have been governed in the event of nuclear attack. Nearby, a colony of rare European yellow-tailed scorpions are said to have recently moved into the yard at Ongar station although nobody seems to know where they actually nest, or how they came to be in the Essex village in the first place.

Sitting in the quiet emptiness of the carriage at Epping it strikes me that tube travel is an oddly singular experience: people do it alone, in vast unconnected swarms. Those neither worrying about being late for their next meeting nor immersed in a newspaper or book are left to daydream. Waiting now for the train to begin its journey back towards West Ruislip, a comforting thought springs to mind. For the entirety of the next fifty minutes, all the way back to Oxford Circus, this seat belongs to me.

The Northern line is an amalgamation of two separate railways: the Hampstead & Highgate (now the Charing Cross branch), and the City & South London, which ran between King William Street and Stockwell (the Bank branch); the latter was the first 'tube' railway in the world, opening in 1890. The line reached its termini at Edgware in 1924, Morden in 1926 and High Barnet in 1940, and currently serves 51 stations over 36 miles. The phrase 'Mind the Gap' has its origins on the line, having first been used on the curved platforms at Embankment.

The original version of the famous London Underground Diagram was designed by Harry Beck in 1931. At the time Beck was a temporary draughtsman with the company – he was reputedly paid five guineas for the job. Today this seems a very small sum for creating what is acknowledged as one of the all-time design classics.

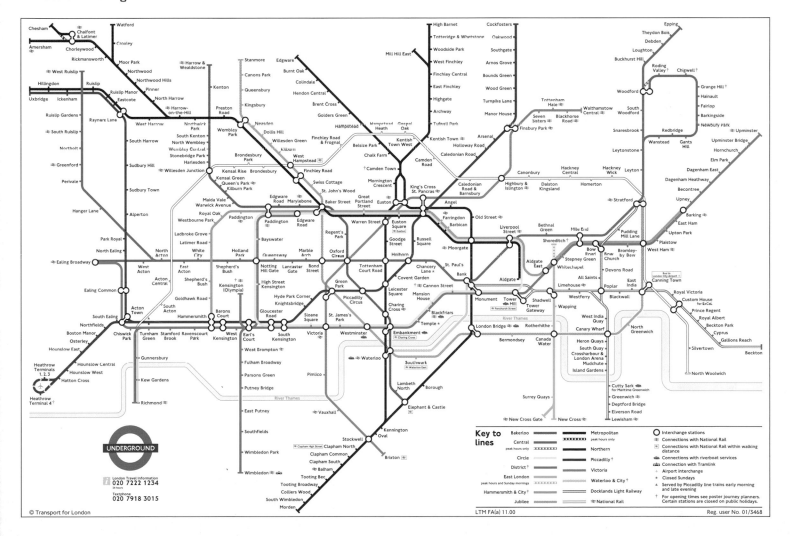

AT 62295

⊖ **Adult**

Name
Mr JAMES.

This photocard is valid for
use only by the person shown with
a ticket bearing the same number

London Transport issued subject to conditions - see over

Simon James moved to London from the Midlands in 1996. Until 1985, when he ran away to art school, he worked as a paramedic technician in the health service. He is presently considering buying an anorak.

More of his photographs can be found at: www.simonjames.co.uk

Special thanks to Mamiya Cameras (Johnsons Photopia Ltd) for the fabulous Mamiya 7 camera used to take all the pictures, to Fuji Photo Film (UK) Ltd for the wonderful Provia 100F transparency film, and to Metro Imaging for handling the processing to their usual high standard of excellence.

Thanks to Richard Atkinson, Clare Baggaley and Stuart Smith, without whose commitment, creativity and patience this book would never have happened, and to Michael Palin for his kind foreword.

Thanks also to my assistants, Anne Golding and Tracy Howl; and last, but in no way least, to Keith Cavanagh, Mike Edwards, Tony Eva, Pejman Faratin, Adonica Gieger, Mark Power, David Sidbury, Piers Smith-Cresswell and Neil Ward for all their help and support.

First published in 2001 by
HarperCollinsPublishers
77-85 Fulham Palace Road
London W6 8JB

The HarperCollins website address is:
www.fireandwater.com

Photographs and text © 2001 Simon James
Foreword © 2001 Michael Palin

Simon James hereby asserts his moral rights to be identified as the author of this work.

London Underground Map by permission of Transport Trading Limited, Registered User No. 01/3468

A CIP catalogue record for this book is available from the British Library.

ISBN: 0 00 711447 8
05 04 03 02 01
9 8 7 6 5 4 3 2

Typeset in Johnston Underground

Design by SMITH

Colour reproduction by Colourscan
Printed and bound by Bath Press Colourbooks